An Analysis of

St. Benedict's

The Rule
of St. Benedict

Benjamin Laird

www.macat.com
info@macat.com

Cover illustration: Capucine Deslouis

Cataloguing in Publication Data
A catalogue record for this book is available from the British Library.
Library of Congress Cataloguing-in-Publication Data is available upon request.

ISBN 978-1-912303-84-7 (hardback)
ISBN 978-1-912127-46-7 (paperback)
ISBN 978-1-912282-72-2 (e-book)

Notice
The information in this book is designed to orientate readers of the work under analysis,
to elucidate and contextualise its key ideas and themes, and to aid in the development
of critical thinking skills. It is not meant to be used, nor should it be used, as a
substitute for original thinking or in place of original writing or research. References and
notes are provided for informational purposes and their presence does not constitute
endorsement of the information or opinions therein. This book is presented solely for
educational purposes. It is sold on the understanding that the publisher is not engaged
to provide any scholarly advice. The publisher has made every effort to ensure that
this book is accurate and up-to-date, but makes no warranties or representations with
regard to the completeness or reliability of the information it contains. The information
and the opinions provided herein are not guaranteed or warranted to produce particular
results and may not be suitable for students of every ability. The publisher shall not be
liable for any loss, damage or disruption arising from any errors or omissions, or from
the use of this book, including, but not limited to, special, incidental, consequential or
other damages caused, or alleged to have been caused, directly or indirectly, by the
information contained within.

CONTENTS

THE MACAT LIBRARY

The Macat Library is a series of unique academic explorations of seminal works in the humanities and social sciences – books and papers that have had a significant and widely recognised impact on their disciplines. It has been created to serve as much more than just a summary of what lies between the covers of a great book. It illuminates and explores the influences on, ideas of, and impact of that book. Our goal is to offer a learning resource that encourages critical thinking and fosters a better, deeper understanding of important ideas.

Each publication is divided into three Sections: Influences, Ideas, and Impact. Each Section has four Modules. These explore every important facet of the work, and the responses to it.

This Section-Module structure makes a Macat Library book easy to use, but it has another important feature. Because each Macat book is written to the same format, it is possible (and encouraged!) to cross-reference multiple Macat books along the same lines of inquiry or research. This allows the reader to open up interesting interdisciplinary pathways.

To further aid your reading, lists of glossary terms and people mentioned are included at the end of this book (these are indicated by an asterisk [*] throughout) – as well as a list of works cited.

Macat has worked with the University of Cambridge to identify the elements of critical thinking and understand the ways in which six different skills combine to enable effective thinking.
Three allow us to fully understand a problem; three more give us the tools to solve it. Together, these six skills make up the **PACIER** model of critical thinking. They are:

ANALYSIS – understanding how an argument is built
EVALUATION – exploring the strengths and weaknesses of an argument
INTERPRETATION – understanding issues of meaning

CREATIVE THINKING – coming up with new ideas and fresh connections
PROBLEM-SOLVING – producing strong solutions
REASONING – creating strong arguments

To find out more, visit **WWW.MACAT.COM.**

CRITICAL THINKING AND *THE RULE OF ST BENEDICT*

Primary critical thinking skill: REASONING
Secondary critical thinking skill: CREATIVE THINKING

The Rule of St Benedict, written around 1500 years ago by the Italian monk St Benedict of Nursia, is a slim handbook for monastic life – a subject many modern readers would regard as relatively niche. It is, however, also a model of the organized and clearly expressed thought produced by good reasoning skills – a mainstay of critical thinking. Reasoning is all about making a good case for something, through logical arguments, neatly and systematically organised. In Benedict's case, his main concern was to lay out a set of rules and practices that would allow monasteries to run as well-organised communities. Communal living presented huge challenges, and yet it was also, Benedict believed, the best way for monks to sustain themselves, their religion, and the learning and teaching that went with it. His Rule laid out concise but detailed chapters on the best way to achieve this, including provisions for all areas of personal and communal discipline, right down to how tasks might be allotted to individual monks. Providing a complete roadmap for successfully running a community, the concise brilliance of *The Rule* has even been suggested by some business professors as useful model for running small businesses today.

ABOUT THE AUTHOR OF THE ORIGINAL WORK

St. Benedict was born in Nursia, in present-day Italy, in 480 C.E. While in Rome pursuing his education, he became frustrated with what he perceived as widespread immorality in the city, and withdrew to become a monk. He would later found several monasteries, including one at Monte Cassino, a rocky hill near Rome, where he spent the rest of his life. St. Benedict died in 547 C.E., but his ideas about communal living and leadership took root, and are still important today.

ABOUT THE AUTHOR OF THE ANALYSIS

Dr Benjamin Laird gained his PhD on the early circulation of St Paul's letters at the University of Aberdeen. He currently teaches in the School of Divinity at Liberty University.

ABOUT MACAT

GREAT WORKS FOR CRITICAL THINKING

Macat is focused on making the ideas of the world's great thinkers accessible and comprehensible to everybody, everywhere, in ways that promote the development of enhanced critical thinking skills.

It works with leading academics from the world's top universities to produce new analyses that focus on the ideas and the impact of the most influential works ever written across a wide variety of academic disciplines. Each of the works that sit at the heart of its growing library is an enduring example of great thinking. But by setting them in context – and looking at the influences that shaped their authors, as well as the responses they provoked – Macat encourages readers to look at these classics and game-changers with fresh eyes. Readers learn to think, engage and challenge their ideas, rather than simply accepting them.

'Macat offers an amazing first-of-its-kind tool for
interdisciplinary learning and research. Its focus on works
that transformed their disciplines and its rigorous approach,
drawing on the world's leading experts and educational institutions,
opens up a world-class education to anyone.'

Andreas Schleicher
Director for Education and Skills, Organisation for Economic
Co-operation and Development

'Macat is taking on some of the major challenges in university
education ... They have drawn together a strong team of active
academics who are producing teaching materials that are
novel in the breadth of their approach.'

Prof Lord Broers,
former Vice-Chancellor of the University of Cambridge

'The Macat vision is exceptionally exciting. It focuses
upon new modes of learning which analyse and explain seminal texts
which have profoundly influenced world thinking and so social and
economic development. It promotes the kind of critical thinking
which is essential for any society and economy.
This is the learning of the future.'

Rt Hon Charles Clarke, former UK Secretary of State for Education

'The Macat analyses provide immediate access to the critical
conversation surrounding the books that have shaped their
respective discipline, which will make them an invaluable resource
to all of those, students and teachers, working in the field.'

Professor William Tronzo, University of California at San Diego

WAYS IN TO THE TEXT

KEY POINTS

- St. Benedict had a significant impact on the lives of monks.
- *The Rule of St. Benedict* is a set of guidelines for how monasteries can be successfully maintained.
- Although it was written in the sixth century, *The Rule of St. Benedict* is still an important text for monks and nuns living today.

Who Was St. Benedict?

St. Benedict was a Christian saint who significantly influenced the development of monasticism,* or monkhood—a practice in which a person relinquishes worldly concerns to focus on religious devotion.

Most of what is known about St. Benedict's early life comes from Pope Gregory the Great,* who was influenced by and wrote about St. Benedict. According to Gregory, St. Benedict was born to a wealthy family in Nursia,* in what is now Italy, around the year 480 C.E. The widespread immorality that he witnessed in Roman culture as a young man drove him to a life of solitude. He later established 12 monastic communities around Subiaco,* a town about 40 miles east of Rome.

St. Benedict spent most of his life at the monastery at Monte Cassino,* a rocky hilltop between Rome and Naples. It was there, after years of experience living in and leading monastic communities, that he wrote *The Rule of St. Benedict,* his most important contribution to monasticism. The book proposes guidelines for operating monasteries and assigns responsibilities to each monk or nun. It quickly became the basis for life in the communities under his care.

Scholars generally agree that St. Benedict died not long after *The Rule* was completed, around the year 543 C.E. In the centuries since his death, monasteries throughout the world have implemented his guidelines.

Today, St. Benedict is considered one of the most important figures in monastic history, and his *Rule* is likely to remain influential in the future.

What Does *The Rule of St. Benedict* Say?

Most scholars agree that St. Benedict wrote *The Rule of St. Benedict* around 540. It comprises 73 chapters, each of which addresses some aspect of monastic living. As a whole, the book shows how monks can live together in permanent, self-sufficient communities. This was an important innovation at the time, as people had disagreed about whether monks should live in isolation or in groups and how groups of monks should organize themselves. St. Benedict's method provided a community structure that was stable and enduring.

The book was also important because it helped monks balance between asceticism*—the practice of denying one's cravings—and personal indulgence. Thus, it benefitted both individuals and entire communities.

Two other aspects of *The Rule* are noteworthy. First, St. Benedict believed that monasteries should choose one of their own members as a leader, what is called an abbot.* Previously, many monasteries had answered to a bishop,* an official of the Roman Catholic Church* who was not a member of the community. This change helped monasteries become more independent. Second, St. Benedict called for monks to perform physical labor in order to assist in the day-to-day maintenance and subsistence of the monastery. That was a change from previous traditions, in which monks were expected to focus on stillness and meditation.

St. Benedict's guidelines were hugely important to the development of monasticism. Never before had anyone written a text that so comprehensively described how to establish and run a permanent monastic community. By the eighth century, monasteries throughout Europe had adopted *The Rule*. It influenced the thinking of many important figures in Christian* history, such St. Boniface,* an eighth-century missionary who helped bring Christianity to what is now Germany; Anselm of Canterbury,* a monk known for his contributions to philosophy in the eleventh and twelfth centuries; and, as mentioned before, Pope Gregory. Since *The Rule*'s initial publication, hundreds of important Christian thinkers have written commentaries on it.

Why Does *The Rule of St. Benedict* Matter?

It speaks to *The Rule*'s importance that it is still relevant today, 1500 years after it was written. Although St. Benedict was not the first monk, people widely acknowledge him as one of the most pivotal figures in the development of monasticism.

Even more important, the thousands of men and women who belong to monastic groups today still use *The Rule of St. Benedict* as a practical guide. Those groups include the Order of St. Benedict,* the Cistercian Order,* and the Order of the Cistercians of Strict Observance, or Trappists.* For them, *The Rule* provides the order and structure necessary for monastic life.

The book has also benefitted men and women who do not belong to a monastery, but who are nevertheless attracted to the lifestyle that *The Rule* describes. In this way, it is relevant for Christians in general, but might also appeal to those who believe in the principles of simplicity and discipline that St. Benedict describes, regardless of their religious beliefs. As such, Christians, historians, those interested in religious studies, and anyone curious about monasticism will find *The Rule* worth reading.

Finally, some people in the business community have recently become interested in *The Rule.* They respect the book for what it can teach business leaders about organization and efficiency.

SECTION 1
INFLUENCES

MODULE 1
THE AUTHOR AND THE HISTORICAL CONTEXT

KEY POINTS

- *The Rule of St. Benedict* is an important text in the history and development of communal monasticism.*

- St. Benedict's view that immorality was widespread in Rome and elsewhere shaped his thinking and work.

- The various forms of monasticism that existed before St. Benedict wrote *The Rule* also influenced him.

Why Read This Text?

St. Benedict's *Rule,* which most scholars agree he wrote around the year 540, significantly affected the development of Christian* monasticism—a way of life that renounces worldly pursuits in favor of service to God. After St. Benedict's death in 543, monasteries throughout the world embraced the guidelines that he set out in *The Rule.* Since then, the book has served as the foundational document for several monastic orders, many of which are still active today.

As philosopher Wil Derkse* writes: "Monastic life remains stubbornly vital. The fifteen-hundred-year-old *Rule of St. Benedict* is used worldwide by tens of thousands of monks and nuns as a guide to their life together. Almost as many and an increasing number of men and women who live outside the monastery have associated themselves as oblate,* associate members, with *The Rule* playing a role in their own conduct of life. This is not about copying the monastic life, but about appropriating it for themselves in a suitable form."[1]

❝ There was a man of venerable life, St. Benedict by name and grace, who from the time of his very childhood carried the heart of an old man. His demeanor indeed surpassing his age, he gave himself no disport [entertainment] or pleasure, but living here upon earth he despised the world with all the glory thereof, at such time as he might have most freely enjoyed it. ❞

Gregory the Great, *The Life of Our Most Holy Father St. Benedict*

Author's Life

Little is known about St. Benedict's background. According to Pope Gregory the Great's* *Dialogues,* which he wrote in 593, St. Benedict was the son of a wealthy family in Nursia,* in what is now Italy. He eventually traveled to Rome to continue his classical education.[2] It is unclear how long he stayed there, but it seems he abandoned his studies after growing tired of what he saw as the decadent culture of the capital. As Gregory writes, St. Benedict was born "of honorable parentage and sent to Rome to continue his classical education. But when he saw there many through the uneven paths of vice run headlong to their own ruin, he drew back his foot, but new-set in the world, lest, in the search of human knowledge, he might also fall into the same dangerous precipice."[3]

Gregory's brief account suggests that St. Benedict turned to a monastic life not because of his education and upbringing, but because of his disdain for the immorality he saw everywhere in Rome. After leaving the city, he traveled west to the town of Subiaco, where he took up residence in a grotto—a cave where a person could live. He stayed there in solitude for three years before helping to establish several monasteries.

Along with other monks, St. Benedict ultimately moved to Monte Cassino,* a rocky hill southeast of Rome, to establish the monastery where he would spend the rest of his life. It was here that he completed *The Rule* around 540. He considered the book to be a basic guide for monastic life.

Author's Background

St. Benedict wrote *The Rule* during the sixth century, when barbaric tribes threatened to invade countries in Western Europe. At this time, the stability of the region was very much in question. In fact, St. Benedict had grown up under the rule of the Ostrogoths,* a group that ruled the Italian peninsula and the Balkan* region during the fifth and sixth centuries. During this tumultuous period, many people were drawn to a life of monasticism. The monastic experience was seen as a chance to retreat from worldly concerns and focus instead on service to God. People pursuing monastic lives considered *The Rule* a valuable resource, and believed its guidelines would help ensure their community's longevity and stability. *The Rule* also helped monks and nuns gain the most benefit from their experience.

St. Benedict was undoubtedly familiar with the more well-known monks who had come before him. By the time he was living, monks such as Paul the Hermit* and Anthony* were already widely regarded as pioneers of the monastic movement. Both Paul and Anthony tended toward extreme asceticism*—the practice of denying physical cravings as an act of devotion to God. They also lived in isolation in remote places.

It wasn't long, however, before monks began organizing themselves into monastic communities. It is likely that Pachomius,* a monk who spent most of his life in Egypt in the fourth century, was the first to organize a monastic community. St. Benedict knew of Pachomius and his efforts to organize a society that retreated from the pressures and temptations of the world to focus exclusively on service to God. He probably developed some of the principles and regulations in the *Rule* based on the lives and work of early monks such as Pachomius. Many of his other ideas came from years of personal experience and interaction with people in his community. While Pachomius and others were responsible for monasticism's early stages, it was St. Benedict who brought order and stability to the movement.

NOTES

1 Wil Derkse, *A Blessed Life: Benedictine Guidelines for Those Who Long for Good Days* (Collegeville: Liturgical Press, 2009), 1–2.

2 For additional background relating to the life of St. Benedict, see Adalbert de Vogüé, *St. Benedict: The Man and His Work*, trans. Gerald Malsbary (Petersham: St. Bede's Publications, 2006); Wyatt North, *The Life and Prayers of Saint Benedict* (Boston: Wyatt North Publishing, 2013); Paschal Cheline, "Christian Leadership: A Benedictine Perspective," *American Theological Library Association Summary of Proceedings* 57 (2003), 107–13.

3 Gregory the Great, *The Life of Our Most Holy Father St. Benedict* (London: Thomas Baker, 1898), introduction.

ACADEMIC CONTEXT

KEY POINTS

- *The Rule of St. Benedict* investigates the purpose of a monastery and how it should function.
- In early Christianity* some monks opted to live in isolation, while others preferred to live in communities.
- St. Benedict was a pioneer of the monastic* movement and provided guidance to people who followed his model.

The Work in its Context

Before the reign of the Roman Emperor Constantine* (306 to 337), Christianity was a small but growing movement that had met with harsh resistance. Many Christians were persecuted for refusing to worship Roman gods and were killed because of their commitment to their faith. Those who died for their commitment were called martyrs, and other Christians held them in high esteem. People came to regard martyrdom* as the ultimate expression of Christian devotion.

After Emperor Constantine converted to Christianity in 313, he legalized the religion throughout the Holy Roman Empire.* Christians experienced less persecution, and monasticism became much more popular. It was considered an ideal way to escape the immorality and distractions of the world and to devote oneself to spiritual growth and service. In response to the increasing popularity of monasticism, St. Benedict wrote *The Rule* as guidance for anybody who committed to a living in a monastery.

All those who joined Benedictine communities were treated equally, regardless of their background. In fact, it wasn't an advantage to be wealthy in a Benedictine monastery, as each monk had to give up his personal possessions when he joined the community.

> ❝ St. Benedict's great contribution was the rule which he gave to his monastery. In devising it he learned what he could from predecessors, especially Basil of Caesarea but also John Cassian, and other monks. However, he was not a slavish borrower, for his rule bears indelibly the mark of his own experience as monk and abbot. ❞
> Kenneth Scott Latourette, *A History of Christianity: Beginnings to 1500*

Overview of the Field

Before St. Benedict, other figures played important roles in developing monasticism. They included John Cassian,* a monk who lived in Bethlehem* and Egypt, and Basil the Great,* a fourth-century church leader who spent much of his life in monastic settings. Also influential was the *Regula Magistri** (Rule of the Master), a sixth-century text that may have served as the basis for the early chapters of *The Rule of St. Benedict*. However, while other people may have first formulated the concept of a monastic community, St. Benedict was most responsible for its growth and development.

St. Benedict lived at a time when several forms of monasticism had already taken shape. In the first chapter of *The Rule*, he describes four main types of monks:

- Cenobites,* who live together in a community and are the type of monk that he had in mind when he wrote *The Rule*
- Anchorites,* who live as hermits in isolation
- Sarabaites,* who live in groups of two or three with little formal discipline or structure
- Landlopers,* who live without formal discipline and travel from place to place, relying on the hospitality of others.

The last two types of monks, according to St. Benedict, are less noble than the first two. After discussing these four types, St. Benedict concludes: "Therefore, passing these over, let us go on with the help of God to lay down a rule for that most valiant kind of monks, the Cenobites."[1]

Academic Influences

St. Benedict was not the first person to live in a monastic setting, nor was he the first to develop guidelines for one. He understood that monasticism was an established tradition and that he played only a part in its development. Other thinkers who came before him certainly influenced him.

It is unclear who specifically made the greatest impression on St. Benedict, although he does mention St. Basil* by name in the final chapter of *The Rule*. Sometimes referred to as Basil the Great, St. Basil lived during the fourth century and was a highly educated Christian leader. He spent several years in monasteries before leading the church of Caesarea, an important Christian community on the Mediterranean Coast in Israel. Basil was known for producing his own guidelines for monastic living, and St. Benedict was undoubtedly aware of them.

St. Benedict was probably also familiar with John Cassian* (c. 360–435), a monk who had spent years in monastic communities in Bethlehem and Egypt. Cassian wrote lengthy discussions about monastic life with which St. Benedict was probably familiar. It is likely that he also knew of the *Regula Magistri* (Rule of the Master), a work that an unknown author in Italy had written early in the sixth century. The prologue of *Regula Magistri* closely mirrors the first seven chapters of St. Benedict's *Rule*.

NOTES

1   Boniface Verheyen, trans., *The Holy Rule of our Most Holy Father St. Benedict* (Atchison: The Abbey Student Press, 1949), 16.

MODULE 3
THE PROBLEM

KEY POINTS

- Before St. Benedict's time, Christian* leaders used a variety of forms and structures to organize monastic* communities.

- While some individuals believed that monks and nuns should live in isolation, others argued for cenobitic,* communal, monasticism.

- St. Benedict believed in cenobitic monasticism and presented guidelines for implementing it.

Core Question

In the centuries after Jesus'* death (c. 30), a few Christians began to retreat from society to dedicate their lives to prayer, meditation, and the study of religious texts. Eventually, some of those early, solitary monks began to travel together and even to form small communities. Initially, they structured and ordered those communities in a variety of ways, with little agreement as to which approach was best. A fundamental question was whether such communities should allow members to live however they pleased or impose specific guidelines.

This question had remained largely unanswered in the sixth century when St. Benedict wrote *The Rule*. The book was important because it provided a balanced model for monastic life. First, it offered structure and discipline to community members without encouraging them toward extreme asceticism*—the practice of denying one's physical cravings and pleasures. Second, *The Rule* showed monks how to run their monasteries in an orderly fashion without dictating the way that they should spend each minute of each day.

> ❝ The collations [writings] of the Fathers, and their
> institutes and lives, and the rule of our Holy Father,
> Basil—what are they but the monuments of the virtues
> of exemplary and obedient monks? ❞
>
> St. Benedict, *The Rule of St. Benedict*

The Participants

St. Benedict was not the first person to live in a monastic setting. For centuries, monks like Anthony the Hermit* (c. 251–356) had lived in isolation, dedicating themselves to spiritual development and contemplation. These monks were known as anchorites,* and they did without many of the conveniences and provisions available at the time. Throughout the fourth and fifth centuries, however, communal monasticism became increasingly popular.

One important founder of early monastic communities was Pachomius* (c. 290–346). Often referred to as the father of cenobitic monasticism, Pachomius is estimated to have overseen 11 monasteries in Egypt during the fourth century, and the traditions he began had immense influence on people in the monastic world, including St. Benedict. He advocated a form of monasticism that was especially rigid and made no allowances for the undisciplined or uncommitted. Yet while St. Benedict certainly recognized the need for order and discipline, he did not believe in a monastic environment that was as severe as those Pachomius designed.

Another of St. Benedict's influences, Basil the Great* (c. 330–379, is mentioned in the final chapter of the *Rule*. Among other things, Basil was known for his ability to properly organize the affairs of local communities and for establishing a number of humanitarian projects. St. Benedict built on Basil's legacy and created a form of monasticism that was well organized and efficient.

The Contemporary Debate

In the first chapter of *The Rule*, St. Benedict identifies several different types of monks. He mentions, for example, those who live as hermits and those who live in small groups and move from location to location. According to St. Benedict, the most honorable monks are those who live in permanent communities, and it was such monks that he hoped to influence through his *Rule*.[1] His intention in writing *The Rule* was not to challenge or criticize others who did not share his beliefs. Instead, he wanted to offer guidance to those who believed as he did that monks should dwell in communities.

Communal monasticism was still developing when St. Benedict wrote *The Rule*. He established his guidelines to offer the structure and stability that he believed were necessary for monastic communities to endure. While many of St. Benedict's principles were unique and innovative, he also incorporated the thinking of other important monks whom he respected. In addition to Basil and Pachomius, St. Benedict was probably familiar with a number of other monastic leaders who preceded him.

NOTES

1   For further discussion of St. Benedict's preference for permanent commitment to a specific monastic community, see Eric Dean, *Saint Benedict for the Laity* (Collegeville: Liturgical Press, 1989), 10–11.

MODULE 4
THE AUTHOR'S CONTRIBUTION

KEY POINTS

- St. Benedict was in favor of a form of monasticism* characterized by obedience to the abbot* and the moderation of basic necessities.

- St. Benedict contributed to the development of monasticism by offering guidelines for the long-term stability of monastic communities.

- Practical concerns, such as how those in his monastic communities should actually live, motivated the work of St. Benedict.

Author's Aims

St. Benedict wrote *The Rule* to offer guidelines for life in a monastery. While each guideline is important, two are particularly noteworthy.

First, perhaps more than any other ancient text, *The Rule* emphasizes the authority of the abbot, the monastery member who is recognized as the leader of the community. According to St. Benedict, the abbot is not merely a spiritual advisor or administrator, but serves in a Jesus Christ*-like role as the authoritative head of the monastery. Each monk is to obey the abbot without question.

As St. Benedict writes in Chapter 2 of the book: "The abbot who is worthy to be over a monastery, ought always to be mindful of what he is called, and make his works square with his name of Superior. For he is believed to hold the place of Christ in the Monastery."[1] Monks or nuns who had moral objections to the abbot's commands could appeal, but otherwise they were to follow his instructions. St. Benedict

> 66 We are, therefore, about to found a school of the Lord's service, in which we hope to introduce nothing harsh or burdensome. But even if, to correct vices or to preserve charity, sound reason dictates anything that turns out somewhat stringent, do not at once fly in dismay from the way of salvation, the beginning of which cannot but be narrow. 99
>
> St. Benedict, *The Rule of St. Benedict*

believed that obeying the abbot was necessary for maintaining the monastery's stability and order, as well as for teaching each monk to live in both humility and submission to God's will.[2]

The second central idea in *The Rule* is that a monastery should permit community members to have only what is necessary for their daily physical needs. For example, it should give the monks and nuns enough food to be well nourished but should not permit them to eat to excess. Similarly, the monks and nuns should not practice any particular activity to the exclusion of other ones. This philosophy was intended to help those in the community to find a balance between asceticism* (the denial of pleasures as an act of devotion to God) and personal indulgence.

After St. Benedict published *The Rule*, a balanced life became the goal of everyone living in Benedictine communities. This concept was at odds with the thinking of many of St. Benedict's predecessors, who had often deprived themselves of basic necessities rather than seek the balanced life that *The Rule* envisioned.

Approach

St. Benedict addressed his *Rule* to monks and nuns living in communities rather than those in solitude or practicing extreme asceticism.* Therefore, many of his guidelines concern the structure of daily community life. Additionally, *The Rule* addresses the lifestyle, behavior, and attitudes that should characterize monks. It also recommends the spiritual disciplines, or exercises intended to foster spiritual development, that they should undertake. While each chapter focuses on a specific subject, together they contain a comprehensive set of guidelines for the all-round life of the monastic community.

Even today, many Christians* regard *The Rule* as a useful means of regulating monastic life and helping monks and nuns progress in their faith. Those who have experienced it will appreciate St. Benedict's aims and intentions, and those who have not will find *The Rule* a helpful introduction to monasticism.

Contribution in Context

After St. Benedict left his studies in Rome, he began his monastic life as a hermit. He would later lead several monastic communities and eventually found his own monasteries. His contemporaries increasingly viewed him as an expert on monastic life, and other Christian leaders came to him for guidance and advice. St. Benedict wrote *The Rule* after several decades of monastic living and hoped it would serve as a guidebook for those who joined his communities.

According to Pope Gregory the Great,* whose own interest in monasticism led him to write about St. Benedict, *The Rule* originated purely out of the concerns of the communities in which St. Benedict lived and served. This is not to say that St. Benedict did not learn from others: he would undoubtedly have been familiar with notable monastic leaders such as John Cassian* and Basil the Great.* However, he probably drew his conclusions more from his practical experiences leading cenobitic* monastic communities than from scholarly debates.

NOTES

1   Boniface Verheyen, trans., *The Holy Rule of our Most Holy Father St. Benedict* (Atchison: The Abbey Student Press, 1949), 16.

2   For a treatment on the importance of humility and submission to the Benedictine way of life, see Michael Casey, *Living in the Truth: Saint Benedict's Teaching on Humility* (Liguori: Liguori Publications, 2001); Thomas Merton, *The Rule of Saint Benedict: Initiation into the Monastic Tradition* (Collegeville: Cistercian Publications, 2009).

SECTION 2
IDEAS

MODULE 5
MAIN IDEAS

KEY POINTS

- St. Benedict's *Rule* provided guidelines for daily life in monastic* communities.
- St. Benedict argued that a monastic community must be properly organized if it is to endure and meet the spiritual needs of its members.
- *The Rule* contains 73 chapters, each of which attends to one particular aspect of life in a monastic community.

Key Themes

St. Benedict's main concern was the spiritual development of those under his care. *The Rule of St. Benedict* is a practical text, and the guidelines it contains are intended to provide stability and order for monastic communities so that those who live in them can focus on progressing in their spiritual journey.

The Rule of St. Benedict comprises a prologue and 73 chapters. Each chapter is brief and relates to a particular aspect of life in a monastic community.[1] Certain chapters deal with subjects like how community members should behave, what responsibilities they have, and what daily provisions they should receive. Some instruct monks on how to pray, meditate, and study. Others make clear the importance of virtues such as humility and obedience. And still others explain important procedures in the community, such as how it should receive new members. Although chapters in *The Rule* sometimes seem unrelated, it is important to remember that St. Benedict arrived at his guidelines after decades of living in monastic settings. His work emerged out of first-hand experience with what he knew to be most important for monastic living.

> **❝** Now, we have written this Rule that, observing it in monasteries, we may show that we have acquired at least some moral righteousness, or a beginning of the monastic life. **❞**
>
> St. Benedict, *The Rule of St. Benedict*

Exploring the Ideas

After living in isolation for three years, St. Benedict relocated with several other monks to a small village southeast of Rome called Monte Cassino,* where he helped establish a monastery. His experience in Monte Cassino persuaded him that communal living was the ideal form of monasticism, but that communities needed structure and organization in order to succeed. To this end, St. Benedict composed *The Rule* as a guide for establishing and managing permanent monastic communities.

The Rule addresses both the practical concerns of running a monastery and the principles and regulations that community members should observe. These regulations include strict obedience to the abbot,* head of the monastery, and a clear description of each member's responsibilities. For example, monks were to perform various physical tasks to keep the monastery functioning and livable. *The Rule* also discusses what provisions each member should receive and the proper means of disciplining disobedient monks.

Language and Expression

St. Benedict wrote *The Rule* in Latin because that was the primary language that people who lived in monastic settings used. However, the book differs from many theological* works in that St. Benedict did not intend it to be for a scholarly audience. Instead, he meant it to serve as a working guide for monastery life.

One consequence of the text being a guide and not an academic work is that it may seem disjointed and disorganized, especially if read as a literary work. As priest and historian Bernard Green observes: "At times, the ordering of the material is confusing. No overall structure is recognizable ... the placing of a number of chapters seems entirely arbitrary.[2]"

While some groups of chapters do seem to share common themes, Green is generally correct. That is because each chapter addresses a distinct subject, and in many cases, people can understand and interpreted it without referring to the others. Exceptions include chapters 8 to 19, which all relate to the daily spiritual disciplines that must be observed, such as the designated times of prayer.[3] Additional groupings include chapters 23 to 29 and 42 to 46, which address how a monastic community should discipline disobedient monks.

NOTES

1   For a more thorough introduction to the structure of the Rule and its main themes, see Adalbert De Vogüé, *The Rule of Saint Benedict: A Doctrinal and Spiritual Commentary* (Collegeville: Cistercian Publications, 1999).

2   Bernard Green, "St. Benedict of Nursia," in *The Encyclopedia of Monasticism: A-L*, ed. William Johnson (New York: Routledge, 2000), 130.

3   As Miriam Schmitt has observed, "In St. Benedict's view all of monastic life is a response to the New Testament precept of 'unceasing prayer,' through which all time is sanctified." Miriam Schmitt, "Benedictine Spirituality," *Liturgical Ministry* 10 (2001), 199.

MODULE 6
SECONDARY IDEAS

KEY POINTS

- St. Benedict argued for strict obedience to the abbot* and a lifetime commitment to the monastery.
- *The Rule* stressed discipline and allegiance to one's monastic community in ways that made it different from other contemporary religious texts.
- Some people have suggested that St. Benedict's *Rule* could also offer useful guidelines in a modern business context.

Other Ideas

While scholars, theologians, and others have widely recognized St. Benedict's *Rule* as influential and important, they have not given some aspects of the text much attention. One such example is St. Benedict's discussion of the abbot's responsibilities and authority. St. Benedict believed that strict obedience to the abbot was vital for the stability of the community.

St. Benedict was also one of the first Christian* leaders to advocate that monks make lifelong commitments to their communities. Before his time, monks travelled frequently and often changed monasteries. St. Benedict believed that such transient and uncommitted members harmed the stability of their communities.

St. Benedict was also concerned about how a monastery should correct disobedient monks. He saw undisciplined monks as threats because they could negatively influence their peers. In chapters 23 to 30,[1] St. Benedict proposes appropriate disciplinary measures and suggests ways that errant monks might restore their good standing in

> 66 The first degree of humility is obedience without delay. This becomes those who, on account of the holy subjection which they have promised, or of the fear of hell, or the glory of life everlasting, hold nothing dearer than Christ. 99
>
> St. Benedict, *The Rule of St. Benedict*

the community. The monastery authority—abbot—should first confront disobedient monks privately, *The Rule* states. If the monk refuses to correct his behavior, the community should expel him.

Exploring the Ideas

In St. Benedict's time, monks lived in a variety of settings, with little agreement as to which was best. As St. Benedict notes in chapter one of *The Rule*, some monks moved from place to place, living off the goodwill of others. St. Benedict, of course, believed that monks were better served by living in permanent communities. As such, *The Rule* was one of the first monastic writings to discourage transient lifestyles, and St. Benedict prescribed strict guidelines for the acceptance of new members.[2]

St. Benedict also believed that a community's stability depended on the authority of an abbot.[3] It is not known whether or not he was the first Christian leader to assign the abbot significant authority; he could have simply drawn on earlier practices in *The Rule*. Further scholarly attention to the development of the abbot's authority would teach us more about both monasticism and the historical significance of the book.

Overlooked

St. Benedict's design of the *Rule* as a guide for monasteries has limited its influence outside of monastic circles. In recent decades, however, some individuals have begun to recognize that those who do not live in monasteries can also learn from *The Rule.*

In her 2003 PhD dissertation, Cheryl Crozier Garcia,* now an associate professor at Hawaii Pacific University, proposes that modern businesses could benefit by implementing Benedictine principles. She writes, "*The Rule of St. Benedict* could be used by privately held, employee-owned corporations with fewer than 100 employees as a guideline for developing an employee code of conduct, recruiting and selection policies, and job descriptions for top corporate executives."[4] According to Crozier, the business community would clearly benefit from *The Rule's* model of leadership.

Quentin Skrabec* similarly suggests that St. Benedict's organizational principles are relevant for today's managers and entrepreneurs. A business professor at the University of Findlay, he writes, "Part of St. Benedict's genius was his integration of community, hierarchy, and organization. St. Benedict's communal organization achieved community goals as well as individual goals."[5] Skrabec argues that one need not live in a monastery to learn from *The Rule.* Even outside a monastic setting, embracing the principles and daily habits that *The Rule* lays out can improve one's religious experiences.

It might have surprised St. Benedict to learn that people who do not live in monasteries have used his *Rule* as a guide. However, given the text's practical insights about the establishment and characteristics of an effective leadership structure, it is understandable that so many people have found the work of St. Benedict worth exploring.

NOTES

1   Passages in the Bible that are of relevance to this topic include Matthew 18:15–20, 1 Corinthians 5:1–13, 2 Corinthians 2:6, and 2 Thessalonians 3:6–15.

2   This may be observed most clearly in Chapter 58 of the *Rule*.

3   St. Benedict discussed the various types of monks in Chapter 1 of *The Rule*.

4   Cheryl Crozier Garcia, "The Use of the Rule of St. Benedict as a Management Model for Secular Organizations" (PhD diss., Walden University, 2003), abstract.

5   Quentin Skrabec, *St. Benedict's Rule for Business Success* (West Lafayette: Purdue University Press, 2003), 15.

MODULE 7
ACHIEVEMENT

KEY POINTS

- **St. Benedict provided practical guidelines for living in a monastic* community, but he most likely intended for it to be used as an introduction, as it did not cover every aspect of a monastic life.**
- **St. Benedict's teachings spread to monasteries around the world and continue to be influential today.**
- **Although *The Rule* was written for those living in monasteries, others have since found it useful, too.**

Assessing the Argument

St. Benedict probably would not have anticipated how influential and lasting *The Rule* would become. And yet, as scholar Eric Dean* observes, "In out-of-the way places here and there throughout the world, there are contemporaries of ours living in a fashion recognizably Benedictine."[1]

Although *The Rule* remains a respected and valued guide, it does not cover every aspect of spirituality and monastic life. St. Benedict probably meant the text as an introduction. For example, in the final chapter of *The Rule,* he writes that the guidelines are useful for acquiring "some moral righteousness, or a beginning of the monastic life." It was only "with God's help" that monks would "attain at last to the greater heights of knowledge and virtue."

St. Benedict acknowledged it was extremely important for each community member to read the Bible, as well as the writings of the Fathers, or early church leaders. *The Rule* alone clearly would not suffice. That said, it is still one of the most important documents of Western monastic history. Many monastic communities active today still look to *The Rule* for guidance.

> **❝** But as we advance in the religious life and faith, we shall run the way of God's commandments with expanded hearts and unspeakable sweetness of love; so that never departing from His guidance and persevering in the monastery in His doctrine till death, we may by patience share in the sufferings of Christ, and be found worthy to be coheirs with Him of His kingdom. **❞**
>
> St. Benedict, *The Rule of St. Benedict*

Achievement in Context

Interest in monastic living increased during the fourth, fifth, and sixth centuries. During that time, Christian* leaders experimented with the form and structure of monastic communities. One reason for *The Rule's* success was that it provided practical answers to questions about how those communities should be organized.

While the communities under the care of St. Benedict adopted *The Rule* quickly, it was probably some time before its influence spread widely. For many centuries, scholars believed that when the Lombards*—a Germanic tribe originally from Scandinavia—invaded Italy in the 570s, Benedictine monks fled to Rome, where they introduced Pope Gregory* to *The Rule*. Pope Gregory then might have sent out monks to introduce Benedictine monasticism wherever the Roman Catholic Church* held influence. This theory seemed plausible because Pope Gregory wrote extensively about St. Benedict in the second book of his *Dialogues,* published in 593.

More recently, however, some people have questioned the depth of Gregory's involvement. Scholar Marilyn Dunn* writes, "Gregory was regarded not as someone who followed *The Rule*, but rather as someone who knew of St. Benedict and recommended his *Rule*." Dunn argues that Gregory should only be understood as "a disciple in the broadest sense of the word."[2]

How quickly *The Rule* spread after St. Benedict wrote it remains unclear. But people were certainly well aware of it by the eighth century, when the powerful European king Charlemagne* became Roman Emperor. Charlemagne decreed that monasteries everywhere in his empire should follow the *Rule*. Even today, *The Rule* continues to influence Benedictine monasteries throughout the world.

Limitations

The main limitation of *The Rule* is that St. Benedict wrote it solely for people committed to life in a monastic community. So despite the text's historical importance, its narrow focus has prevented it from reaching a large audience or receiving much analysis or criticism. Most opposition to the text is philosophical: not all who commit themselves to monasticism agree with St. Benedict's teachings. For example, some monks live in isolation, while others live in small groups that do not answer to an abbot.

It is worth noting that readers who do not live in monasteries have recently begun to see *The Rule* as a valuable practical and spiritual guide. One of the attractions of monasticism is that it offers people the chance to become part of a stable community. Therefore, while St. Benedict wrote the text for Christians, readers of other backgrounds can learn from the permanence and stability that characterize monastic life. And, of course, many monasteries around the world today follow Benedict's *Rule*. This shows that the text is valuable to Christians regardless of their cultural or geographical background.

NOTES

1   Eric Dean, "St. Benedict's Way: A Protestant Appraisal of Monasticism," *Encounter* 31:4 (1970), 325.

2   Marilyn Dunn, *The Emergence of Monasticism: From the Desert Fathers to the Early Middle Ages* (Oxford: Blackwell, 2003), 131.

MODULE 8
PLACE IN THE AUTHOR'S WORK

KEY POINTS

- *The Rule of St. Benedict* is the only surviving known work of St. Benedict.
- *The Rule* represents the mature thinking of St. Benedict.
- *The Rule* solidified St. Benedict's reputation as a key figure in monastic history.

Positioning

When he was young, St. Benedict left his studies to live as a hermit at Subiaco,* a town east of Rome. Later, he would travel southwest to establish a monastery at Monte Cassino.* By the time he wrote *The Rule*, St. Benedict had spent about 40 years in monastic settings like these. Such experiences made him aware of the challenges that monastic communities faced, and he tried to develop guidelines that would benefit both individual monks and communities as a whole. The result was *The Rule*—the culmination of his life's work and reflection. In it, we find the teachings of a seasoned, mature monk.

Although some scholars suggest that St. Benedictine published *The Rule* as early as 520, most believe he finished it around 540, about a decade before his death. Unfortunately, nothing else he may have written has survived.

Integration

It is important to take St. Benedict's life experiences into account when considering why he wrote *The Rule*. According to *Dialogues*, the second book of Pope Gregory the Great,* St. Benedict left his hometown of Nursia* and traveled south to Rome to continue his

> **" Listen, O my son, to the precepts of your master, and incline the ear of your heart, and cheerfully receive and faithfully execute the admonitions of your loving Father, that by the toil of obedience you may return to Him from whom by the sloth of disobedience you have gone away. "**
>
> St. Benedict, *The Rule of St. Benedict*

classical education. In the city, he encountered what he thought was widespread immorality, and he eventually left to focus on his spiritual development in solitude. Later, St. Benedict relocated to Monte Cassino,* 80 miles to the south of Rome, where he helped found a monastery. He spent the rest of his life there, and his experiences as a monastic leader shaped the guidelines found in *The Rule*.

People should view the work as a response to practical dilemmas that monastic leaders faced rather than a product of intellectual curiosity. St. Benedict's original readers were those who joined one of his monasteries—not scholars or unaffiliated Christians. Each provision in *The Rule* addresses a particular need in the monastic community, and the work as a whole is intended to help monasteries survive without having to depend on the Roman Catholic Church* or the towns in which they are located.

Significance

St. Benedict would not have regarded himself as an author or an academic. He wrote *The Rule* near the end of his life to help the communities under his care succeed and endure. *The Rule* is his lone surviving work and the basis of his fame.

After St. Benedict's death, monastic communities warmly received *The Rule*. According to scholar James Smith,* several monasteries in modern-day France and Great Britain had implemented its guidelines by the seventh century. In addition, in the eighth century, the Roman Emperor Charlemagne* decreed that monasteries throughout the Roman Empire should follow *The Rule.*[1] Today, many monasteries in the Roman Catholic and Greek Orthodox* traditions still abide by *The Rule*'s guidelines.

The Rule succeeded for a number of reasons. It garnered praise initially because many people had great respect for St. Benedict. Even when he was young, people often approached him for guidance and instruction. In fact, one reason he began establishing monastic communities was because so many individuals wanted to learn from him. Many Christians also believed that St. Benedict performed miracles, and that naturally increased the demand for his teaching.

The Rule has also been successful because it is practical. St. Benedict had years of experience living in and leading monasteries, and the guidelines he offered were not merely theoretical or ideological.*

Furthermore, *The Rule* did not advocate the harsh asceticism* (the practice of denying physical cravings and pleasures as an act of devotion to God) that some monks practiced, especially those who lived in isolation. For some readers, *The Rule*'s guidelines about the harsh discipline of errant monks, and the requirements for daily religious activities, may seem strict or excessive by today's standards. However, it is important to remember that St. Benedict's aim was to aid each member of the community in their spiritual journey. As Benedictine scholar Pavel Chelline* writes, St. Benedict believed that "discipline is an absolute for one who is going to conform his life to the pattern given by the Gospel."[2]

NOTES

1   James Smith, "Benedictines," in *The Dictionary of Historical Theology*, ed. Trevor Hart (Grand Rapids: Eerdmans, 2000), 64.

2   Paschal Cheline, "Christian Leadership: A Benedictine Perspective," *American Theological Library Association Summary of Proceedings* 57 (2003), 109.

SECTION 3
IMPACT

MODULE 9
THE FIRST RESPONSES

KEY POINTS

- *The Rule* has been criticized for overemphasizing the abbot's* authority and the importance of physical labor.
- Not everyone agrees with St. Benedict that monks should live in permanent communities.
- The Reformation* of the sixteenth century and the subsequent split in the Christian Church lessened the influence of Benedictine monasteries.

Criticism

Historically, one of the most controversial aspects of *The Rule* is that it encouraged each community to select an abbot as leader. Previously, monasteries had often been governed by local bishops* who were not community members. Many monasteries adopted St. Benedict's policy because it helped them maintain stability.

The role of the abbot changed after an important historical gathering of religious officials, known as the Fourth Council of the Lateran,* that convened in Rome in 1215. More than a thousand bishops, monks, and other church representatives took part. Among the council's decrees were that all monasteries in a local province form a single congregation, and that abbots should refrain from performing duties for which regular church officials were typically responsible. In many cases, these rulings led to a reduced role for Benedictine abbots.

Another criticism of *The Rule* is that it puts too much emphasis on physical labor. Some monasteries have modified and even ignored St. Benedict's stipulation that all monks should perform physical tasks. For St. Benedict, daily physical work was necessary for the survival of the

> **❝** Idleness is the enemy of the soul; and therefore the brethren ought to be employed in manual labor at certain times, at others, in devout reading. **❞**
>
> St. Benedict, *The Rule of St. Benedict*

monastery and complemented prayer and study. Wealthy monasteries, however, were able to hire local workers so that monks were free to pursue other interests. One such example is the monastery founded in the tenth century by Berno* in Cluny, France. While Berno mostly followed *The Rule,* his monks were permitted not to do physical labor. It was this sort of lax application of Benedictine rules that led to the founding of the Cistercian Order* in the eleventh century. Cistercian monasteries are known for their strict adherence to the letter of *The Rule*.

Responses

Because St. Benedict's *Rule* was written so long ago (in approximately 540), little is known about the criticisms it initially received. We do know, however, that not all readers would have agreed with St. Benedict's monastic philosophy.

For example, in the first chapter of *The Rule*, St. Benedict identifies four distinct types of monks—Cenobites,* Anchorites,* Sarabaites,* and Landlopers.*[1] Cenobitic monks live in communities under the rule of an abbot. Anchorites were hermits—monks living in isolation. Sarabaites lived in small, unstructured groups, and Landlopers roamed from place to place, living off the hospitality of others. While St. Benedict had little regard for Sarabaites or Landlopers, he did respect those who lived as hermits and practiced extreme asceticism,* denying themselves all physical pleasures as an act of devotion to God. Nevertheless, he regarded monks who lived in permanent communities, Cenobites, as the "most valiant kind of monks."

These descriptions suggest that while the majority of sixth-century Christians may have had great respect for St. Benedict, not all were drawn to the communal nature of Benedictine monasticism. Unfortunately, we have no historical evidence of how people whose convictions differed from *The Rule* responded to it.

Conflict and Consensus

As an ancient text, the reception of St. Benedict's *Rule* is best measured by how much it has influenced monastic communities throughout history. That said, there are a few reasons why St. Benedict never entered into scholarly debate with those who disagreed with *The Rule.* One is simply that he died not long after finishing the work. Another reason is that, because *The Rule* was a practical text and not an academic treatise, those who disagreed with it would have responded by adopting a different approach to monastic living rather than by criticizing the work in writing,

Although *The Rule* has always been valuable to the monastic community, its influence has changed over the centuries. One significant event in the history of monasticism was the Protestant Reformation* of the sixteenth century. The most important leader of the Reformation, a former monk named Martin Luther,* challenged the supreme authority of the papacy*—the office of the Pope—and caused a major split in the Christian Church. Following the Reformation, many Christians in Europe joined Protestant churches, and the number and influence of Benedictine monasteries was diminished.

NOTES

1   As Marilyn Dunn notes, St. Benedict's identification of four distinct forms of monasticism seems to have been inspired by John Cassian's work known as *Conference Eighteen*. In this work, Cassian identified the same types of monks as did St. Benedict. Marilyn Dunn, *The Emergence of Monasticism: From the Desert Fathers to the Early Middle Ages* (Oxford: Blackwell, 2003), 115.

MODULE 10
THE EVOLVING DEBATE

KEY POINTS

- Although *The Rule of St. Benedict* has always been influential, some communities have changed or overlooked parts of it.
- *The Rule of St. Benedict* is now important to not only monks, but also Christian* scholars.
- Today, observers of *The Rule* include monastic communities such as the Order of St. Benedict,* the Cistercian Order,* and the Order of Cistercians of the Strict Observance (Trappists*).

Uses and Problems

Historically, St. Benedict's *Rule* has been one of the most influential guides to monastic living, and Benedictine communities have generally followed the text closely. However, over the last 1,500 years, some monasteries have relaxed their adherence to certain parts of it.[1]

Some monasteries, for example, have hired local workers to perform the physical labor that *The Rule* says should be carried out by monks. This was the case with the abbey in Cluny,* France, though its founder, Berno,* otherwise followed *The Rule*. In addition, while *The Rule* called for monasteries to be independent, with one of their own members (the abbot) in charge, they have at times failed to maintain such independence and been placed in regional congregations with a common leader.

Schools of Thought

Today, those who follow *The Rule* include the Order of St. Benedict, the Cistercian Order, and the Order of Cistercians of the Strict

> **❝** After his death his style of monasticism continued as only a local phenomenon in Italy. Only gradually did the Benedictines become an outward-looking movement with principles that caught on over a much larger area. **❞**
>
> Ivor Davidson, *A Public Faith*

Observance (often called Trappists).[2] For monks and nuns who belong to these orders, *The Rule* is central to everyday life and plays an important role in their intellectual development.

Scholars are also interested in *The Rule*. While they were not St. Benedict's intended audience, the book is important to historians of Christianity,* as well as to those interested in the history of monasticism. Some people have also tried to incorporate principles from *The Rule* into their everyday lives, observing a daily schedule that includes specific times for prayer and study and a healthy balance of physical and mental work.

In Current Scholarship

Over the last 1,500 years, theologians, historians, and religious leaders—including several Popes of the Roman Catholic Church*— have emerged from Benedictine communities. A few notable examples include St. Boniface,* an eighth-century missionary who helped bring Christianity to what is now Germany; the scholarly monk St. Bede,* also known as the Venerable Bede, who wrote an extensive volume on English history during the eighth century; and Anselm of Canterbury,* a monk known for his contributions to philosophy.

In addition, several distinct monastic orders continue to follow *The Rule*. The largest and most influential of these is the Order of St. Benedict (OSB), a group that has been practicing Benedictine traditions since it began in the sixth century. Other Benedictine monks who wanted to follow *The Rule* more closely founded the Cistercian Order in the eleventh century. A particular branch of the Cistercians emerged in the 1600s in France and is known for its extraordinarily strict adherence to *The Rule*. Called the Trappists, these monks have even invented their own sign language so that they do not need to speak aloud. They follow this practice, while not prescribed in *The Rule*, in order to provide an atmosphere conducive to study and meditation.

Although people have adapted *The Rule* to a variety of contexts since its publication, its place in the monastic tradition remains strong. Monasteries will undoubtedly continue to follow its guidelines in the future.

NOTES

1   Sergio Zincone, "St. Benedict of Nursia," in *Encyclopedia of Ancient Christianity Volume One: A-E*, ed. Angelo Di Berardino (Downers Grove: InterVarsity Press, 2014), 352–3.

2   For a brief overview of the various orders within the Benedictine tradition, see, James Smith, "Benedictines," in *The Dictionary of Historical Theology*, ed. Trevor Hart (Grand Rapids: Eerdmans, 2000), 64–5.

MODULE 11
IMPACT AND INFLUENCE TODAY

KEY POINTS

- Today, *The Rule of St. Benedict* is important to monastic* communities and to people drawn to the lifestyle that the book promotes.

- St. Benedict did not write *The Rule* to challenge any particular theories about monasticism.

- Scholars today continue to discuss exactly how St. Benedict wrote *The Rule*, as well as who influenced him in writing it.

Position

St. Benedict wrote *The Rule* to provide order and stability for communities under his care, and the book influenced monastic communities for nearly 1,500 years. After its publication in 540, monasteries throughout Europe widely embraced it. The Protestant Reformation* in the sixteenth century—after which many Catholic monasteries were either abandoned, destroyed, or fell into decline— somewhat checked the book's influence. Yet it should be noted that this was because of resistance to the Roman Catholic Church,* not to *The Rule* itself.

Even after the Reformation, *The Rule* is still a foundational text for today's monastic communities. It is also an important historical text, as it tells us much about early monasticism. For example, the first chapter of *The Rule* shows that some monks lived in isolation, while others lived in communities.

Finally, *The Rule* is an important guide to spirituality and daily living. The book can even be helpful to people who do not live in

> 66 You, therefore, who hold to the heavenly home, with the help of Christ fulfill this least rule written for a beginning; and then you shall with God's help attain at last to the greater heights of knowledge and virtue which we have mentioned above. 99
>
> St. Benedict, *The Rule of St. Benedict*

monasteries by providing practical guidelines related to study, religious practices, and daily activities.

Interaction

St. Benedict did not write *The Rule* to challenge a particular theory of monasticism or the views of other monastic leaders. Instead, he wanted to show how to organize life in a monastery. The form of monasticism he favored was unique during his time. Years of experience had shown him that monks should devote themselves to living at one monastery for the stability and longevity of the community.

He also wrote that the ultimate authority in each monastery was the abbot,* who was a member of the community. This was an important change from the common practice at the time, which was for monasteries to operate under the authority of a local bishop*—an official of the Roman Catholic Church. Bishops who operated monasteries often ran them as extensions of the Church instead of autonomous, or self-sufficient communities, as St. Benedict believed they should be.

Finally, *The Rule* differed from previous monastic approaches because it called for each monk or nun to perform physical labor each day. Before St. Benedict's time, many monks and nuns lived in solitude, devoting their time and energy to study, prayer, and meditation. However, St. Benedict recognized that physical labor could be a healthy complement to religious activities.

The Continuing Debate

Historians continue to debate *The Rule*'s origins. One important question is whether the version of *The Rule* that we read today reflects the original draft, or whether St. Benedict actually wrote the final chapters. Although no one has found ancient manuscripts that prove the original text was shorter, many scholars now agree that chapters 67 to 73 were written later.

Chapter 66 concludes, "But we desire that this Rule be read quite often in the community, that none of the brethren may excuse himself of ignorance." That has prompted scholars like Wil Derkse* to claim that it was the text's original ending. Derkse writes: "This [the conclusion of chapter 66] suggests that St. Benedict is finished. However, in the final version another seven chapters follow, about matters which he had not thought about."[1] Benedictine scholar Adalbert de Vogüé* agrees. He writes: "In its original form, *The Rule of St. Benedict*, like that of the Master, came to an end with the chapter on the gatekeepers or porters… The phrasing of St. Benedict has the sound of a conclusion, confirming the suspicion that *The Rule* ended here in its first edition."[2]

Church historians have also debated *The Rule*'s influences. It is widely recognized that St. Benedict based some of his beliefs on the writings of two men: Basil the Great,* a fourth-century Christian leader who spent many years in monastic settings, and John Cassian,* a monk who spent much of his life in Egypt, and who, like Basil, wrote about his experiences. Less clear is the relationship between St. Benedict's *Rule* and the *Regula Magistri** (Rule of the Master), an anonymously written sixth-century work that looked to regulate monastic life. Although it was once believed that the *Regula Magistri* was written after *The Rule*, historians now think that St. Benedict drew inspiration from it.[3]

The majority of people who have written about *The Rule* have been members of the Order of St. Benedict* (OSB). However, because members of Benedictine communities tend not to engage with the scholarly community, no specific individuals are seen as representative of the field.

NOTES

1   Wil Derkse, *A Blessed Life: Benedictine Guidelines for Those Who Long for Good Days* (Collegeville: Liturgical Press, 2009), xi.

2   Adalbert de Vogüé, *St. Benedict: The Man and His Work*, trans. Gerald Malsbary (Petersham: St. Bede's Publications, 2006), 103.

3   Sergio Zincone, "St. Benedict of Nursia," in *Encyclopedia of Ancient Christianity Volume One: A-E*, ed. Angelo Di Berardino (Downers Grove: InterVarsity Press, 2014), 352–3.

MODULE 12
WHERE NEXT?

KEY POINTS

- *The Rule* will probably continue to be important for monastic* communities in the future, although changing legal codes mean that people will now read certain elements of it differently.

- *The Rule* can also benefit individuals who do not live in monastic communities but nevertheless find St. Benedict's principles personally enriching.

- The fact that *The Rule* has endured as an important text about monasticism that people still follow to this day makes it an important work.

Potential

People have used *The Rule* as a guide for monastic life for many centuries, and we have no reason to believe that this will change soon. For the most part, the book's guidelines are no longer a topic of scholarly debate. However, portions of the text are sometimes altered or read differently according to who reads them and when. For example, St. Benedict wrote that boys could be admitted to the monastery if certain requirements were fulfilled. Today, the legal rights of the boy's relatives, as well as local and national laws, complicate this particular rule.

While the text is mainly read by monastic communities, people who do not live in monasteries have begun to find it important. Many have recently come to recognize *The Rule* as an excellent guide to Christian living. If this trend continues, *The Rule* could enjoy a wider audience in the future.[1]

> **"** The principle merit of St. Benedict's *Rule* seems to have been its elaboration of a synthesis [fusion] of previous monastic experience, showing great wisdom, moderation, and balance in the organization of cenobitic life. **"**
>
> Sergio Zincone, "St. Benedict of Nursia"

Future Directions

St. Benedict's *Rule* has played a significant role in the history of monasticism and of Christianity* in general. As the historian and Benedictine monk Bernard Green* has observed, "Almost the whole history of Western monasticism for the last thousand years has been a series of revivals and reinterpretations of *The Rule*."[2] In the future, *The Rule* will continue to shape and regulate Christian monasticism.

In addition to monks and historians, others have recently begun to see *The Rule* as a guide for Christian spirituality. Some of these new readers are unaffiliated with a particular monastery, and others, sometimes called oblates,* have aligned themselves with the traditions of a monastic order, although they do not live in a monastery. Regardless of their background, these new readers feel they can benefit from following *The Rule*'s principles.

Summary

In the fourth and fifth centuries when St. Benedict lived, monasticism was still being developed. His *Rule* outlined a communal type of monasticism that struck a balance between personal freedom and extreme asceticism.* Many monasteries adopted *The Rule* for its practical value, and because people greatly admired St. Benedict.

Although he was not the first to establish a monastic community, St. Benedict contributed significantly to monasticism's development. His book was the first to call for the rule of an abbot* in each monastery. It was also one of the first texts to require monks to make lifelong commitments to their monasteries. Finally, *The Rule* is known for valuing physical labor. Monks were not to spend their lives in stillness and quiet study, but to do work that sustained the monastery.

The Rule of St. Benedict deserves special attention for its historical significance. Its contribution is still apparent today, as monastic communities around the world follow its guidelines, and even Christians who are not members of monasteries turn to it for personal enrichment. St. Benedict's work ensured that his monasteries would succeed and endure, and provided guidelines to help each member progress in his or her spiritual development.

NOTES

1   For a discussion of the possible ways in which individuals living in greater society may incorporate Benedictine principles into their daily lives, see Terrence Kardong, *Conversation with Saint Benedict: The Rule in Today's World* (Collegeville: Liturgical Press, 2012).

2   Bernard Green, "St. Benedict of Nursia," in *The Encyclopedia of Monasticism: A-L*, ed. William Johnston (New York: Routledge, 2000), 132.

GLOSSARY

GLOSSARY OF TERMS

Abbot: member of a monastery who is recognized as the leader of the community.

Anchorites: monks who lived as hermits in isolation, especially in Egypt from the first through fourth centuries.

Asceticism: the practice of denying physical cravings and pleasures as an act of devotion to God and as a means of progressing in religious virtues.

Balkans: the region encompassing southeast Europe. The area includes the modern-day country of Greece as well as several of the neighboring countries to the north.

Bethlehem: small village in the modern-day West Bank of Israel that is the traditional site of the births of King David and Jesus.

Bishop: high-ranking Christian leader who typically had authority over several churches in a local region.

Cenobites: monks who live in a monastic community and share a common life.

Christianity: religion founded upon the person and teachings of Jesus, a first-century Jew from the city of Nazareth.

Cistercian Monastic Order: Roman Catholic monastic order founded in the late-eleventh century in France. The order is known for their strict adherence to *The Rule of St. Benedict*.

Fourth Council of the Lateran (1215): a meeting of over a thousand religious officials convened by Pope Innocent III to assess the impact of the Fourth Crusade's (1202–04) failure, which resulted in the loss of Constantinople.

Greek Orthodox Church: ancient body of churches that does not recognize the authority of the Bishop of Rome. The church is most influential in Greece and countries in Eastern Europe.

Holy Roman Empire: major political power in central Europe from the tenth through the nineteenth centuries composed of several territories.

Ideology: set of beliefs, usually religious or political, that influence one's ambitions and decisions.

Landloper: a monk who lives without discipline and travels from place to place, taking advantage of the hospitality of others.

Lombards: Germanic people, originally from Scandinavia, who migrated south. The Lombards held power over the Italian peninsula from the late-sixth through late-eighth centuries.

Martyrdom: the act of dying for one's cause, especially one's religious beliefs.

Monasticism: the practice of living either in isolation or within a specific community in order to carry out specific religious convictions. Monastic communities often live by specific guidelines and require their members to take certain vows.

Monte Cassino: a small town about 80 miles southeast of Rome. St. Benedict helped establish a monastery in this location on top of a rocky cliff.

Nursia: a small Italian town to the northeast of Rome and the birthplace of St. Benedict. Also spelled "Norcia."

Oblate: someone who has committed to monastic principles but lives in society rather than in a monastic setting.

Order of St. Benedict (OSB): Roman Catholic monastic order that traces its history to the sixth century and follows *The Rule of St. Benedict*.

Ostrogoths: group that ruled the Italian peninsula and the Balkan region during the fifth and sixth centuries and played a significant role in the decline of the Roman Empire.

Papacy: the office of the Pope. The Pope is the Bishop of Rome and the head of the Roman Catholic Church. According to the Church, the Pope is a successor of the apostle Peter, one of the original followers of Jesus.

Protestant Reformation: theological disputes that took place in the sixteenth century in Europe that led to a split in Christendom. At the center of controversy was the authority of the papacy and the doctrine of salvation. Those who broke away from the Roman Catholic Church were known as Protestants.

Regula Magistri **(Rule of the Master):** a work written by an anonymous author in Italy early in the sixth century. It is believed that this text influenced St. Benedict's thinking.

Roman Catholic Church: a major institution within Christianity headed by the Bishop of Rome, also known as the Pope.

Sarabaites: monks who lived prior to the sixth century in groups of two or three with little discipline or structure.

Subiaco: a town located about 40 miles east of Rome.

Theology: the study of God (His attributes and works). In a more general sense, theology includes the study of the teachings of a particular religion.

Trappists: also known as the Order of Cistercians of the Strict Observance. The order is a branch of the Cistercian Order that strictly observes St. Benedict's *Rule*. The order was founded in the seventeenth century in France. Among other things, the order is known for inventing its own sign language so that members would not have to speak.

PEOPLE MENTIONED IN THE TEXT

Anselm of Canterbury (c. 1033–1109) was a Benedictine monk, philosopher, and Church prelate, who held the office of Archbishop of Canterbury from 1093 to 1109.

Anthony the Hermit (251–356) was one of the earliest Christians to leave society in order to live in solitude and asceticism. Many early Christians who sought a similar lifestyle looked to him for inspiration and guidance.

Basil the Great (330–379) was a bishop of Caesarea, modern-day Turkey. Basil was one of the first to advocate communal monasticism.

Bernard Green (1953–2013) was a historian and Benedictine monk in the Ampleforth Abbey in England.

Berno (c. 850–927) was a member of the monastery in Cluny, France during the tenth century. He was known for founding the monastery and for his adherence to Benedictine monasticism.

John Cassian (c. 360–435) was a monk who favored an Egyptian-style monasticism, which was characterized by strict discipline. Cassian's writings are thought to have influenced St. Benedict.

Charlemagne (d. 814) was declared Holy Roman Emperor on Christmas day of the year 800 by Pope Leo III. At the time of his death, his empire had extended to much of Western Europe.

Paschal Cheline (1936–2015) was for many years a monk and theologian at Mount Angel Abbey in Oregon.

Constantine (c. 272–337) was a Roman Emperor from 306–37. He was the first emperor to convert to Christianity.

Eric Dean (1924–89) served as a Presbyterian minister and was a professor of Humanities at Wabash College.

Wil Derkse (b. 1952) is a Dutch philosopher who teaches at the Radboud University in the Netherlands.

Marilyn Dunn is a senior lecturer in medieval history at the University of Glasgow, Scotland.

Cheryl Crozier Garcia is currently an associate professor at the College of Professional Studies of Hawaii Pacific University.

Gregory the Great (c. 540–604) also known as Pope Gregory I, was an influential pope who was attracted to monasticism and thus to St. Benedict. He wrote *Dialogues* in approximately 593.

Jesus Christ of Nazareth: is believed to have been the Son of God, his teachings serve as the basis for Christianity. When he was 33, the Roman army captured and crucified him, after which he resurrected and ascended to heaven.

Martin Luther (1483–1546) was a former Augustinian monk and a key leader in the Protestant Reformation. He was also one of the first to translate the Bible into German.

Pachomius (c. 290–346) is thought to be the first monk to develop a monastic community. Pachomius oversaw several monasteries in Egypt, and his thinking influenced many in the monastic tradition, including St. Benedict.

Paul the Hermit (229–c.340) was one of the first Christian monks to live in isolation. Also known as Paul of Thebes, he lived in the Egyptian desert and is regarded as a pioneer of monasticism.

Quentin Skrabec is a professor of business at the University of Findlay.

James Smith is a lecturer in theology at Loyola University in Chicago.

St. Bede (c. 673–735) was an English monk, theologian, and historian, who is better known as the Venerable Bede. He is best known for writing *The Ecclesiastical History of the English People*, which serves as a primary source for the early history of England.

St. Boniface (672–754) was an Anglo-Saxon missionary, who helped spread Christianity in Germany.

Adalbert de Vogüé (1924–2011) was a French Benedictine monk and historian of Benedictine Christianity.

WORKS CITED

WORKS CITED

Casey, Michael. *Living in the Truth: Saint Benedict's Teaching on Humility*. Liguori: Liguori Press, 2001.

Cheline, Paschal. "Christian Leadership: A Benedictine Perspective." *American Theological Library Association Summary of Proceedings* 57 (2003): 107–13.

Chittister, Joan. *The Rule of St. Benedict: A Spirituality for the 21st Century*. New York: The Crossroad Publishing Company, 2010.

Wisdom Distilled from the Daily: Living the Rule of St. Benedict Today. New York: HarperOne, 2009.

Davidson, Ivor. *A Public Faith: From Constantine to the Medieval World: AD 312-600*. Grand Rapids: Baker, 2005.

Derkse, Wil. *A Blessed Life: Benedictine Guidelines for Those Who Long for Good Days*. Collegeville: Liturgical Press, 2009.

De Vogüé, Adalbert. *A Critical Study of the Rule of St. Benedict: Volume 1: Overview*. Hyde Park, NY: New City Press, 2013.

Reading Saint Benedict: Reflections on the Rule. Collegeville: Liturgical Press, 1994.

St. Benedict: The Man and His Work. Translated by Gerald Malsbary. Petersham: St. Bede's Publications, 2006.

The Rule of Saint Benedict: A Doctrinal and Spiritual Commentary. Collegeville: Cistercian Publications, 1999.

De Waal, Esther. *Seeking God: The Way of St. Benedict*. Collegeville: Liturgical Press, 1984.

Dean, Eric. *Saint Benedict for the Laity*. Collegeville: Liturgical Press, 1989.

"St. Benedict's Way: A Protestant Appraisal of Monasticism." *Encounter* 31:4 (1970): 325–37.

Dunn, Marilyn. *The Emergence of Monasticism: From the Desert Fathers to the Early Middle Ages*. Oxford: Blackwell, 2003.

Eberle, Luke, editor. *The Rule of the Master*. Kalamazoo: Cistercian Publications, 1977.

Garcia, Cheryl Crozier. "The Use of the Rule of St. Benedict as a Management Model for Secular Organizations." PhD diss., Walden University, 2003.

Green, Bernard. "St. Benedict of Nursia." In *Encyclopedia of Monasticism: A-L*, edited by William Johnston. New York: Routledge, 2000.

Gregory the Great. *The Life of Our Most Holy Father St. Benedict*. London: Thomas Baker, 1898.

Holzherr, George. *The Rule of Saint St. Benedict: A Guide to Christian Living*. Dublin: Four Courts Press, 1994.

Kardong, Terrence G. *St. Benedict's Rule: A Translation and Commentary*. Collegeville: Liturgical Press, 1996.

Conversation with Saint Benedict: The Rule in Today's World. Collegeville: Liturgical Press, 2012.

Latourette, Kenneth Scott. *A History of Christianity. Volume I: Beginnings to 1500*. Peabody: Prince Press, 2000.

Merton, Thomas. *The Rule of Saint Benedict: Initiation into the Monastic Tradition*. Collegeville: Cistercian Publications, 2009.

North, Wyatt. *The Life and Prayers of Saint Benedict*. Boston: Wyatt North Publishing, 2013.

Schmitt, Miriam. "Benedictine Spirituality." *Liturgical Ministry* 10 (2001): 198–200.

Skrabec, Quentin. *St. Benedict's Rule for Business Success*. West Lafayette: Purdue University Press, 2003.

Smith, James. "Benedictines." In *The Dictionary of Historical Theology*, edited by Trevor Hart. Grand Rapids: Eerdmans, 2000.

Verheyen, Boniface, trans. *The Holy Rule of our Most Holy Father St. Benedict*. Atchison: The Abbey Student Press, 1949.

Zincone, Sergio. "St. Benedict of Nursia." In *Encyclopedia of Ancient Christianity Volume One: A-E*, edited by Angelo Di Berardino. Downers Grove: InterVarsity Press, 2014.

THE MACAT LIBRARY
BY DISCIPLINE

AFRICANA STUDIES

Chinua Achebe's *An Image of Africa: Racism in Conrad's Heart of Darkness*
W. E. B. Du Bois's *The Souls of Black Folk*
Zora Neale Huston's *Characteristics of Negro Expression*
Martin Luther King Jr's *Why We Can't Wait*
Toni Morrison's *Playing in the Dark: Whiteness in the American Literary Imagination*

ANTHROPOLOGY

Arjun Appadurai's *Modernity at Large: Cultural Dimensions of Globalisation*
Philippe Ariès's *Centuries of Childhood*
Franz Boas's *Race, Language and Culture*
Kim Chan & Renée Mauborgne's *Blue Ocean Strategy*
Jared Diamond's *Guns, Germs & Steel: the Fate of Human Societies*
Jared Diamond's *Collapse: How Societies Choose to Fail or Survive*
E. E. Evans-Pritchard's *Witchcraft, Oracles and Magic Among the Azande*
James Ferguson's *The Anti-Politics Machine*
Clifford Geertz's *The Interpretation of Cultures*
David Graeber's *Debt: the First 5000 Years*
Karen Ho's *Liquidated: An Ethnography of Wall Street*
Geert Hofstede's *Culture's Consequences: Comparing Values, Behaviors, Institutes and Organizations across Nations*
Claude Lévi-Strauss's *Structural Anthropology*
Jay Macleod's *Ain't No Makin' It: Aspirations and Attainment in a Low-Income Neighborhood*
Saba Mahmood's *The Politics of Piety: The Islamic Revival and the Feminist Subject*
Marcel Mauss's *The Gift*

BUSINESS

Jean Lave & Etienne Wenger's *Situated Learning*
Theodore Levitt's *Marketing Myopia*
Burton G. Malkiel's *A Random Walk Down Wall Street*
Douglas McGregor's *The Human Side of Enterprise*
Michael Porter's *Competitive Strategy: Creating and Sustaining Superior Performance*
John Kotter's *Leading Change*
C. K. Prahalad & Gary Hamel's *The Core Competence of the Corporation*

CRIMINOLOGY

Michelle Alexander's *The New Jim Crow: Mass Incarceration in the Age of Colorblindness*
Michael R. Gottfredson & Travis Hirschi's *A General Theory of Crime*
Richard Herrnstein & Charles A. Murray's *The Bell Curve: Intelligence and Class Structure in American Life*
Elizabeth Loftus's *Eyewitness Testimony*
Jay Macleod's *Ain't No Makin' It: Aspirations and Attainment in a Low-Income Neighborhood*
Philip Zimbardo's *The Lucifer Effect*

ECONOMICS

Janet Abu-Lughod's *Before European Hegemony*
Ha-Joon Chang's *Kicking Away the Ladder*
David Brion Davis's *The Problem of Slavery in the Age of Revolution*
Milton Friedman's *The Role of Monetary Policy*
Milton Friedman's *Capitalism and Freedom*
David Graeber's *Debt: the First 5000 Years*
Friedrich Hayek's *The Road to Serfdom*
Karen Ho's *Liquidated: An Ethnography of Wall Street*

John Maynard Keynes's *The General Theory of Employment, Interest and Money*
Charles P. Kindleberger's *Manias, Panics and Crashes*
Robert Lucas's *Why Doesn't Capital Flow from Rich to Poor Countries?*
Burton G. Malkiel's *A Random Walk Down Wall Street*
Thomas Robert Malthus's *An Essay on the Principle of Population*
Karl Marx's *Capital*
Thomas Piketty's *Capital in the Twenty-First Century*
Amartya Sen's *Development as Freedom*
Adam Smith's *The Wealth of Nations*
Nassim Nicholas Taleb's *The Black Swan: The Impact of the Highly Improbable*
Amos Tversky's & Daniel Kahneman's *Judgment under Uncertainty: Heuristics and Biases*
Mahbub Ul Haq's *Reflections on Human Development*
Max Weber's *The Protestant Ethic and the Spirit of Capitalism*

FEMINISM AND GENDER STUDIES

Judith Butler's *Gender Trouble*
Simone De Beauvoir's *The Second Sex*
Michel Foucault's *History of Sexuality*
Betty Friedan's *The Feminine Mystique*
Saba Mahmood's *The Politics of Piety: The Islamic Revival and the Feminist Subject*
Joan Wallach Scott's *Gender and the Politics of History*
Mary Wollstonecraft's *A Vindication of the Rights of Women*
Virginia Woolf's *A Room of One's Own*

GEOGRAPHY

The Brundtland Report's *Our Common Future*
Rachel Carson's *Silent Spring*
Charles Darwin's *On the Origin of Species*
James Ferguson's *The Anti-Politics Machine*
Jane Jacobs's *The Death and Life of Great American Cities*
James Lovelock's *Gaia: A New Look at Life on Earth*
Amartya Sen's *Development as Freedom*
Mathis Wackernagel & William Rees's *Our Ecological Footprint*

HISTORY

Janet Abu-Lughod's *Before European Hegemony*
Benedict Anderson's *Imagined Communities*
Bernard Bailyn's *The Ideological Origins of the American Revolution*
Hanna Batatu's *The Old Social Classes And The Revolutionary Movements Of Iraq*
Christopher Browning's *Ordinary Men: Reserve Police Batallion 101 and the Final Solution in Poland*
Edmund Burke's *Reflections on the Revolution in France*
William Cronon's *Nature's Metropolis: Chicago And The Great West*
Alfred W. Crosby's *The Columbian Exchange*
Hamid Dabashi's *Iran: A People Interrupted*
David Brion Davis's *The Problem of Slavery in the Age of Revolution*
Nathalie Zemon Davis's *The Return of Martin Guerre*
Jared Diamond's *Guns, Germs & Steel: the Fate of Human Societies*
Frank Dikotter's *Mao's Great Famine*
John W Dower's *War Without Mercy: Race And Power In The Pacific War*
W. E. B. Du Bois's *The Souls of Black Folk*
Richard J. Evans's *In Defence of History*
Lucien Febvre's *The Problem of Unbelief in the 16th Century*
Sheila Fitzpatrick's *Everyday Stalinism*

The Macat Library By Discipline

Eric Foner's *Reconstruction: America's Unfinished Revolution, 1863-1877*
Michel Foucault's *Discipline and Punish*
Michel Foucault's *History of Sexuality*
Francis Fukuyama's *The End of History and the Last Man*
John Lewis Gaddis's *We Now Know: Rethinking Cold War History*
Ernest Gellner's *Nations and Nationalism*
Eugene Genovese's *Roll, Jordan, Roll: The World the Slaves Made*
Carlo Ginzburg's *The Night Battles*
Daniel Goldhagen's *Hitler's Willing Executioners*
Jack Goldstone's *Revolution and Rebellion in the Early Modern World*
Antonio Gramsci's *The Prison Notebooks*
Alexander Hamilton, John Jay & James Madison's *The Federalist Papers*
Christopher Hill's *The World Turned Upside Down*
Carole Hillenbrand's *The Crusades: Islamic Perspectives*
Thomas Hobbes's *Leviathan*
Eric Hobsbawm's *The Age Of Revolution*
John A. Hobson's *Imperialism: A Study*
Albert Hourani's *History of the Arab Peoples*
Samuel P. Huntington's *The Clash of Civilizations and the Remaking of World Order*
C. L. R. James's *The Black Jacobins*
Tony Judt's *Postwar: A History of Europe Since 1945*
Ernst Kantorowicz's *The King's Two Bodies: A Study in Medieval Political Theology*
Paul Kennedy's *The Rise and Fall of the Great Powers*
Ian Kershaw's *The "Hitler Myth": Image and Reality in the Third Reich*
John Maynard Keynes's *The General Theory of Employment, Interest and Money*
Charles P. Kindleberger's *Manias, Panics and Crashes*
Martin Luther King Jr's *Why We Can't Wait*
Henry Kissinger's *World Order: Reflections on the Character of Nations and the Course of History*
Thomas Kuhn's *The Structure of Scientific Revolutions*
Georges Lefebvre's *The Coming of the French Revolution*
John Locke's *Two Treatises of Government*
Niccolò Machiavelli's *The Prince*
Thomas Robert Malthus's *An Essay on the Principle of Population*
Mahmood Mamdani's *Citizen and Subject: Contemporary Africa And The Legacy Of Late Colonialism*
Karl Marx's *Capital*
Stanley Milgram's *Obedience to Authority*
John Stuart Mill's *On Liberty*
Thomas Paine's *Common Sense*
Thomas Paine's *Rights of Man*
Geoffrey Parker's *Global Crisis: War, Climate Change and Catastrophe in the Seventeenth Century*
Jonathan Riley-Smith's *The First Crusade and the Idea of Crusading*
Jean-Jacques Rousseau's *The Social Contract*
Joan Wallach Scott's *Gender and the Politics of History*
Theda Skocpol's *States and Social Revolutions*
Adam Smith's *The Wealth of Nations*
Timothy Snyder's *Bloodlands: Europe Between Hitler and Stalin*
Sun Tzu's *The Art of War*
Keith Thomas's *Religion and the Decline of Magic*
Thucydides's *The History of the Peloponnesian War*
Frederick Jackson Turner's *The Significance of the Frontier in American History*
Odd Arne Westad's *The Global Cold War: Third World Interventions And The Making Of Our Times*

LITERATURE

Chinua Achebe's *An Image of Africa: Racism in Conrad's Heart of Darkness*
Roland Barthes's *Mythologies*
Homi K. Bhabha's *The Location of Culture*
Judith Butler's *Gender Trouble*
Simone De Beauvoir's *The Second Sex*
Ferdinand De Saussure's *Course in General Linguistics*
T. S. Eliot's *The Sacred Wood: Essays on Poetry and Criticism*
Zora Neale Huston's *Characteristics of Negro Expression*
Toni Morrison's *Playing in the Dark: Whiteness in the American Literary Imagination*
Edward Said's *Orientalism*
Gayatri Chakravorty Spivak's *Can the Subaltern Speak?*
Mary Wollstonecraft's *A Vindication of the Rights of Women*
Virginia Woolf's *A Room of One's Own*

PHILOSOPHY

Elizabeth Anscombe's *Modern Moral Philosophy*
Hannah Arendt's *The Human Condition*
Aristotle's *Metaphysics*
Aristotle's *Nicomachean Ethics*
Edmund Gettier's *Is Justified True Belief Knowledge?*
Georg Wilhelm Friedrich Hegel's *Phenomenology of Spirit*
David Hume's *Dialogues Concerning Natural Religion*
David Hume's *The Enquiry for Human Understanding*
Immanuel Kant's *Religion within the Boundaries of Mere Reason*
Immanuel Kant's *Critique of Pure Reason*
Søren Kierkegaard's *The Sickness Unto Death*
Søren Kierkegaard's *Fear and Trembling*
C. S. Lewis's *The Abolition of Man*
Alasdair MacIntyre's *After Virtue*
Marcus Aurelius's *Meditations*
Friedrich Nietzsche's *On the Genealogy of Morality*
Friedrich Nietzsche's *Beyond Good and Evil*
Plato's *Republic*
Plato's *Symposium*
Jean-Jacques Rousseau's *The Social Contract*
Gilbert Ryle's *The Concept of Mind*
Baruch Spinoza's *Ethics*
Sun Tzu's *The Art of War*
Ludwig Wittgenstein's *Philosophical Investigations*

POLITICS

Benedict Anderson's *Imagined Communities*
Aristotle's *Politics*
Bernard Bailyn's *The Ideological Origins of the American Revolution*
Edmund Burke's *Reflections on the Revolution in France*
John C. Calhoun's *A Disquisition on Government*
Ha-Joon Chang's *Kicking Away the Ladder*
Hamid Dabashi's *Iran: A People Interrupted*
Hamid Dabashi's *Theology of Discontent: The Ideological Foundation of the Islamic Revolution in Iran*
Robert Dahl's *Democracy and its Critics*
Robert Dahl's *Who Governs?*
David Brion Davis's *The Problem of Slavery in the Age of Revolution*

The Macat Library By Discipline

Alexis De Tocqueville's *Democracy in America*
James Ferguson's *The Anti-Politics Machine*
Frank Dikotter's *Mao's Great Famine*
Sheila Fitzpatrick's *Everyday Stalinism*
Eric Foner's *Reconstruction: America's Unfinished Revolution, 1863-1877*
Milton Friedman's *Capitalism and Freedom*
Francis Fukuyama's *The End of History and the Last Man*
John Lewis Gaddis's *We Now Know: Rethinking Cold War History*
Ernest Gellner's *Nations and Nationalism*
David Graeber's *Debt: the First 5000 Years*
Antonio Gramsci's *The Prison Notebooks*
Alexander Hamilton, John Jay & James Madison's *The Federalist Papers*
Friedrich Hayek's *The Road to Serfdom*
Christopher Hill's *The World Turned Upside Down*
Thomas Hobbes's *Leviathan*
John A. Hobson's *Imperialism: A Study*
Samuel P. Huntington's *The Clash of Civilizations and the Remaking of World Order*
Tony Judt's *Postwar: A History of Europe Since 1945*
David C. Kang's *China Rising: Peace, Power and Order in East Asia*
Paul Kennedy's *The Rise and Fall of Great Powers*
Robert Keohane's *After Hegemony*
Martin Luther King Jr.'s *Why We Can't Wait*
Henry Kissinger's *World Order: Reflections on the Character of Nations and the Course of History*
John Locke's *Two Treatises of Government*
Niccolò Machiavelli's *The Prince*
Thomas Robert Malthus's *An Essay on the Principle of Population*
Mahmood Mamdani's *Citizen and Subject: Contemporary Africa And The Legacy Of
Late Colonialism*
Karl Marx's *Capital*
John Stuart Mill's *On Liberty*
John Stuart Mill's *Utilitarianism*
Hans Morgenthau's *Politics Among Nations*
Thomas Paine's *Common Sense*
Thomas Paine's *Rights of Man*
Thomas Piketty's *Capital in the Twenty-First Century*
Robert D. Putman's *Bowling Alone*
John Rawls's *Theory of Justice*
Jean-Jacques Rousseau's *The Social Contract*
Theda Skocpol's *States and Social Revolutions*
Adam Smith's *The Wealth of Nations*
Sun Tzu's *The Art of War*
Henry David Thoreau's *Civil Disobedience*
Thucydides's *The History of the Peloponnesian War*
Kenneth Waltz's *Theory of International Politics*
Max Weber's *Politics as a Vocation*
Odd Arne Westad's *The Global Cold War: Third World Interventions And The Making Of Our Times*

POSTCOLONIAL STUDIES

Roland Barthes's *Mythologies*
Frantz Fanon's *Black Skin, White Masks*
Homi K. Bhabha's *The Location of Culture*
Gustavo Gutiérrez's *A Theology of Liberation*
Edward Said's *Orientalism*
Gayatri Chakravorty Spivak's *Can the Subaltern Speak?*

PSYCHOLOGY

Gordon Allport's *The Nature of Prejudice*
Alan Baddeley & Graham Hitch's *Aggression: A Social Learning Analysis*
Albert Bandura's *Aggression: A Social Learning Analysis*
Leon Festinger's *A Theory of Cognitive Dissonance*
Sigmund Freud's *The Interpretation of Dreams*
Betty Friedan's *The Feminine Mystique*
Michael R. Gottfredson & Travis Hirschi's *A General Theory of Crime*
Eric Hoffer's *The True Believer: Thoughts on the Nature of Mass Movements*
William James's *Principles of Psychology*
Elizabeth Loftus's *Eyewitness Testimony*
A. H. Maslow's *A Theory of Human Motivation*
Stanley Milgram's *Obedience to Authority*
Steven Pinker's *The Better Angels of Our Nature*
Oliver Sacks's *The Man Who Mistook His Wife For a Hat*
Richard Thaler & Cass Sunstein's *Nudge: Improving Decisions About Health, Wealth and Happiness*
Amos Tversky's *Judgment under Uncertainty: Heuristics and Biases*
Philip Zimbardo's *The Lucifer Effect*

SCIENCE

Rachel Carson's *Silent Spring*
William Cronon's *Nature's Metropolis: Chicago And The Great West*
Alfred W. Crosby's *The Columbian Exchange*
Charles Darwin's *On the Origin of Species*
Richard Dawkin's *The Selfish Gene*
Thomas Kuhn's *The Structure of Scientific Revolutions*
Geoffrey Parker's *Global Crisis: War, Climate Change and Catastrophe in the Seventeenth Century*
Mathis Wackernagel & William Rees's *Our Ecological Footprint*

SOCIOLOGY

Michelle Alexander's *The New Jim Crow: Mass Incarceration in the Age of Colorblindness*
Gordon Allport's *The Nature of Prejudice*
Albert Bandura's *Aggression: A Social Learning Analysis*
Hanna Batatu's *The Old Social Classes And The Revolutionary Movements Of Iraq*
Ha-Joon Chang's *Kicking Away the Ladder*
W. E. B. Du Bois's *The Souls of Black Folk*
Émile Durkheim's *On Suicide*
Frantz Fanon's *Black Skin, White Masks*
Frantz Fanon's *The Wretched of the Earth*
Eric Foner's *Reconstruction: America's Unfinished Revolution, 1863-1877*
Eugene Genovese's *Roll, Jordan, Roll: The World the Slaves Made*
Jack Goldstone's *Revolution and Rebellion in the Early Modern World*
Antonio Gramsci's *The Prison Notebooks*
Richard Herrnstein & Charles A Murray's *The Bell Curve: Intelligence and Class Structure in American Life*
Eric Hoffer's *The True Believer: Thoughts on the Nature of Mass Movements*
Jane Jacobs's *The Death and Life of Great American Cities*
Robert Lucas's *Why Doesn't Capital Flow from Rich to Poor Countries?*
Jay Macleod's *Ain't No Makin' It: Aspirations and Attainment in a Low Income Neighborhood*
Elaine May's *Homeward Bound: American Families in the Cold War Era*
Douglas McGregor's *The Human Side of Enterprise*
C. Wright Mills's *The Sociological Imagination*

The Macat Library By Discipline

Thomas Piketty's *Capital in the Twenty-First Century*
Robert D. Putman's *Bowling Alone*
David Riesman's *The Lonely Crowd: A Study of the Changing American Character*
Edward Said's *Orientalism*
Joan Wallach Scott's *Gender and the Politics of History*
Theda Skocpol's *States and Social Revolutions*
Max Weber's *The Protestant Ethic and the Spirit of Capitalism*

THEOLOGY

Augustine's *Confessions*
Benedict's *Rule of St Benedict*
Gustavo Gutiérrez's *A Theology of Liberation*
Carole Hillenbrand's *The Crusades: Islamic Perspectives*
David Hume's *Dialogues Concerning Natural Religion*
Immanuel Kant's *Religion within the Boundaries of Mere Reason*
Ernst Kantorowicz's *The King's Two Bodies: A Study in Medieval Political Theology*
Søren Kierkegaard's *The Sickness Unto Death*
C. S. Lewis's *The Abolition of Man*
Saba Mahmood's *The Politics of Piety: The Islamic Revival and the Feminist Subject*
Baruch Spinoza's *Ethics*
Keith Thomas's *Religion and the Decline of Magic*

COMING SOON

Chris Argyris's *The Individual and the Organisation*
Seyla Benhabib's *The Rights of Others*
Walter Benjamin's *The Work Of Art in the Age of Mechanical Reproduction*
John Berger's *Ways of Seeing*
Pierre Bourdieu's *Outline of a Theory of Practice*
Mary Douglas's *Purity and Danger*
Roland Dworkin's *Taking Rights Seriously*
James G. March's *Exploration and Exploitation in Organisational Learning*
Ikujiro Nonaka's *A Dynamic Theory of Organizational Knowledge Creation*
Griselda Pollock's *Vision and Difference*
Amartya Sen's *Inequality Re-Examined*
Susan Sontag's *On Photography*
Yasser Tabbaa's *The Transformation of Islamic Art*
Ludwig von Mises's *Theory of Money and Credit*